◆ F I R S T ◆ A C T I O N ◆ S K I L L S ◆

Swimming

Marit Claridge

Contents

Edited by Mike Halson and Stella Love
Designed by Anne McCaig
Illustrated by Brian Salmon

Swimming advice by Crystal Palace National Sports Centre
Action photography by Ocean Optics Ltd.

The publishers would like to thank all those who gave their assistance in making this book, and
especially Lisa Busby, Donna Carpenter, Yasmin Gabr, Patrick Harrop, Darren Hicks,
Carina Southward, Susie Stephenson.

INTRODUCING SWIMMING

Everyone can enjoy swimming, no matter how young or old they are or whether they swim in a swimming pool or in the sea. Some people swim because it is a fun way to keep fit and supple. Some like to join clubs and compete in races while others find that learning to swim leads on to all sorts of other exciting watersports such as water polo, synchronized swimming or even windsurfing, water skiing, scuba diving and many others.

This book shows you how to do the basic swimming strokes – front crawl, breast stroke and back crawl. There are exercises to practise the correct arm and leg movements, and photographs showing you how they fit together into a smooth, continuous movement through the water. There is no real order for learning the strokes, so do whichever one you find easiest.

The last part of the book tells you about diving and suggests some games and acrobatics you can try in the water. There is also a section about going further and playing water polo or doing synchronized swimming and some information about the swimming awards you can work towards.

You will need a grown up who can swim well to help you learn to swim. If your school does not run swimming lessons, go to your local pool and find out what classes they run.

Once you have learnt to swim, there are lots of exciting games you can play.

EQUIPMENT

All you need to go swimming is a costume and towel but you might want to use some of the other things shown on this page. You might use armbands or buoyancy aids when you first start to learn, but floats and goggles can be useful even when you are a good swimmer.

Rinse and dry your costume after use.

Don't forget to take your towel.

Goggles stop the chemicals (which keep the pool water clean) from stinging your eyes.

A cap keeps hair dry and out of the way.

Floats are often used for training.

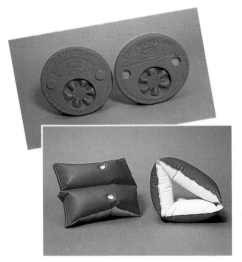

◄ **Armbands and buoyancy aids help you to float when you are a beginner.**

▲
Ball games are fun to play in the pool.

FIRST THINGS FIRST

If you have never been in a swimming pool before, go along and have a look at your local pool. Find out when the pool is very busy and choose a quiet time to go for your first swim. Take your time getting used to the water and just enjoy walking, splashing and jumping in the pool. Later you will learn the basic skills of floating, sculling and gliding.

Entering the pool

Climb BACKWARDS down the steps into the shallow end of the pool. In later visits to the pool, you can try different ways of entering the water. From sitting on the edge, gently lower yourself into the water by twisting round and taking the weight on your hands, as shown in the pictures below. Then stand at the edge and step into the water. Later, try jumping in. You can see how to dive in on pages 22-25.

◀ Put your hands across your body onto the side. Turn round, take your weight on your hands and lower yourself into the water.

Climbing out

Try to climb out of the pool without using the steps. Place both hands on the poolside, shoulder-width apart. Push off from the bottom of the pool, and take your weight onto your arms, keeping your elbows high. Straighten your arms and bring one knee up onto the side.

Getting used to the water

Walk around with your shoulders under the water, sliding your feet along the bottom of the pool.

When you feel ready, hold on to your teacher's hands, or the rail at the side of the pool and jump up and down. How high up can you jump?

Learning to float

Take two floats and put one under each armpit. Lift your feet off the bottom of the pool by pulling your knees up towards your chest. Hold your feet up for as long as you can, then put them down again. Repeat this a few times and hold your feet up a little longer each time.

Floating and sculling

When you can float easily using the floats, try again without them. You may find it difficult to begin with, but it will soon get easier.

Stretch your arms out a little way from your sides, with the palms of your hands facing down. Make small, flat figures of eight with your hands and arms to help you get into your floating position and then keep you there. This is called sculling.

Stretch out wide to make a star.

Pull your knees towards your chest.

Making shapes

See how many different shapes you can make in the water – stretch out your arms and legs as wide as you can to make a star. Stretch your body into a long arrow. Stand up after each shape you make by lifting your head, pushing down on the floats and tucking your legs back underneath your body.

You can use the sculling action to move forwards and backwards too. To move head first, scull as before but with your fingers tilted upwards.

To go feet first, scull with your fingers pointing to the bottom of the pool.

Standing up

Without floats to push against you will need to use your arms to help you to stand up.

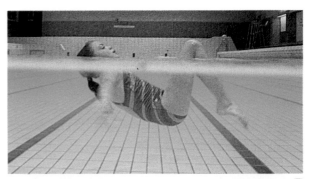

1 On your front

Press down with your hands as you lift your head and bend your knees. As your body becomes upright, push your feet down and stand. Use your hands for balance.

2 On your back

Lift your head forwards, press down and back with your hands and bring your knees up towards your chest. As you tip forwards give an extra push forwards and up with your hands before pushing your feet down to stand.

Gliding

With a push off from the side of the pool, you can glide on your back and your front.

Back glide

Holding on to the rail at the side of the pool, place your feet on the wall as shown in the picture.

Let go of the rail and push off with your feet into a glide.

Front glide

Position yourself at the side of the pool, as shown in the picture.

Push off from the wall with both feet, bringing your arms around in front of your head. Keep your face underwater.

When you have slowed down, stand up as shown on page 7.

Link-up exercise

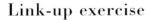

Do the following exercise to link up some of the swimming skills you have learnt so far.

Push off from the side of the pool into a glide on your front.

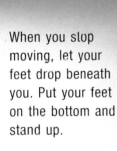

When you stop moving, let your feet drop beneath you. Put your feet on the bottom and stand up.

Lift your feet up again to float on your back, sculling to keep your balance. Scull yourself forwards and backwards.

Treading water

Treading water is a useful skill to learn for playing water games and for water safety. When you are ready to swim in deeper water, try floating in an upright position by sculling with your arms and kicking with your feet.

Sit in the water as if you are on a bicycle. Start cycling your legs and scull with your hands flat.

LEARNING THE CRAWL

Body position

Your body should be as flat as possible with your eyes looking forwards and downwards. Your feet should remain just under the surface. Your body will roll a bit during the stroke due to the alternating arm action and breathing.

Entry

Your hand goes into the water, thumb first, arm bent slightly at the elbow. Once in the water stretch your arm and turn the palm of your hand to face your feet.

Pull

Your arm pulls down and back and your elbow bends more until your hand is under your body and your upper arm is at right angles to your body.

Push

Then your hand starts to push backwards and slightly outwards. As your hand pushes back, straighten your arm slowly until your thumb is alongside your thigh.

Arm movements

Your arms take it in turn to pull through the water in a continuous movement. One arm pulls down and back through the water while the other returns to the front, elbow high in the air, to go into the water again.

Leg movements

The main job of your legs in crawl is to keep your body stable and balanced. They take it in turn to kick up and down – one leg is up whilst the other is down. The kick starts at your hips then down through slightly bent knees and ends with a whip-like action of your foot.

Return

Lift your arm out of the water, elbow first. Keep your bent elbow high in the air as you swing your arm forward. Your hand passes close to your head ready to enter the water again.

Timing your breathing

It is important to time your breathing, so it does not spoil the flow of the stroke.

Your head turns as your elbow begins to lift out of the water. Take a quick breath and turn your head back to the front before your arm enters the water. Breathe out slowly into the water.

Crawl leg movements

Start by gliding on your front, holding a float in front of you. Kick your legs up and down, bending a little at the knees, and you will move forwards through the water.

Keep your legs long, toes pointed and try to kick from the top of your legs rather than just your feet. Try also lying on your back and kicking. Hold the float close to your chest or scull with your hands if you can manage without the float.

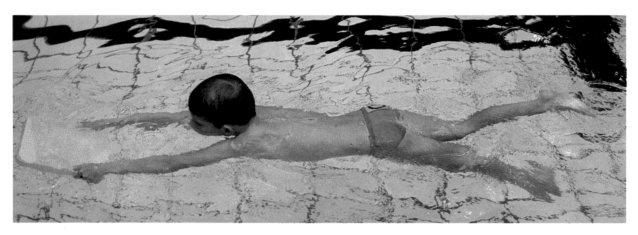

Dog paddle

Now, without a float, glide on your front. Stretch and pull your arms back under your body at the same time as kicking your feet. Your hands should feel as if they are pushing the water backwards, underneath and behind you.

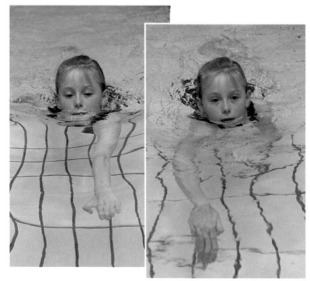

Stretch and pull ▶

Keep your hands under ◀ the water.

Crawl arms

On pages 10 and 11 you can see how the arms move in crawl. The best way to start learning is as shown below.

Stand at least waist deep in the water, with one foot in front of the other. Lean forward and practise the complete arm movement.

Now push off from the side of the pool and start kicking your legs. Do a stroke with each arm. Try again – do two and then three strokes. See how many you can do.

Breathing

In crawl, you swim with your face in the water. To breathe in, you turn your head to one side as your arm is coming out of the water. You can turn your head to either side, whichever feels best.

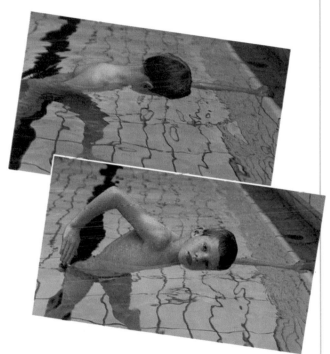

Practise crawl breathing by standing at the edge of the pool. Stretch one arm out and hold the rail. Lean forwards with your face in the water. Turn your head to the side, away from your arm, and take a quick breath in. Put your face back in the water and breathe out slowly. Repeat until this kind of breathing seems easy to you.

LEARNING THE BREAST STROKE

You may wish to learn the breast stroke before crawl as you can see where you are going and you can keep your head above the water to begin with.

The wedge kick

There are two types of breast stroke kick. The first one is the WEDGE KICK. You can practise this swimming on your front or your back. Look at the pictures, then sit at the side of the pool and try the kick.

Now try the kick in the water, using a float. Hold the float out in front and push off into a front glide. See how far you can go in one kick.

▲
Make your feet long and pointed.

▲
Once you have pulled your knees up, turn your feet out.

From the glide position, bend your knees up and out, bringing the soles of your feet almost together.

Now turn your feet out like a frog, keeping your feet flat.

Kick your legs out to a wedge shape. Push your heels back, bringing your legs together to point your toes.

Next, practise the kick again, but on your back. Hold one float under each arm and look at your feet.

Arm movements

There are two kinds of arm action in breast stroke – STRAIGHT ARM and BENT ARM. First of all, practise the straight arm action in shallow water, with your shoulders just above the surface. Start by holding your arms out in front, in the glide position, with your hands flat.

With your arms straight, pull them down and back underwater to a wide V-shape.

Bend and drop your elbows and move your hands together.

Stretch out into the glide position again.

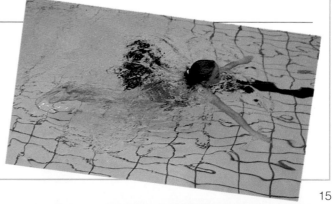

Now try linking these movements. Push off from the side into a front glide. As your elbows drop, your knees start bending up. Kick your legs and stretch your arms out to glide.

Body position

Your body should be as flat as possible. This is easier if you put your face in the water while you are gliding.

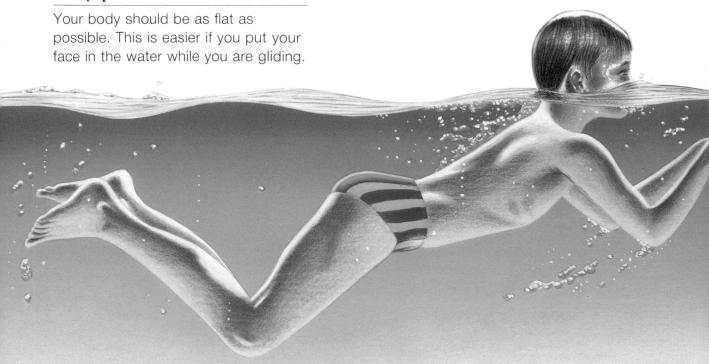

Leg movements

The second type of kick is called the WHIP KICK. It is faster than the wedge kick and is used in swimming races.

Both types of breast stroke leg kick are strong and should give you a big push through the water.

Whip kick

The whip kick works like the wedge kick, but when your knees are bent it does not look so frog-like. Start in a glide position.

Arm movements

The arm action in breast stroke is a non-stop circling movement with a short glide. This can be done with straight or bent arms. On page 15 you started with straight arms. The bent arm action is faster and goes best with the whip kick.

Bent arm action

Begin with your arms stretched out in front of you, hands touching.

Start pulling your arms out and back, bending your elbows as you do so.

Bring your hands back together in a prayer position and stretch out smoothly into a glide.

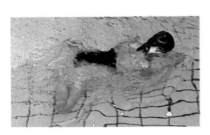 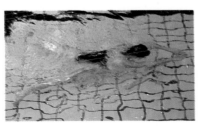

Bend your knees down. Bring your heels up to your bottom, hip-width apart, and the soles of your feet to the surface.

Turn your feet out. Keeping them flat, push mainly backwards in a slight curve. Finish by pointing your toes.

Putting the stroke together

Bring your heels up towards your bottom whilst your arms are pulling back. Kick your legs just as your arms move back into the glide position.

Legs begin to kick back, as arms stretch into glide.

Breathing

If you wish, you can keep your head out of the water all the time in breast stroke. But if you do put your face in the water for most of the stroke it will help you swim faster.

▲
Lift your head and breathe in after you have pulled your arms back.

▲
Put your face in the water and breathe out as you push your hands back into the glide position.

LEARNING THE BACK CRAWL

Back crawl is very like front crawl. Your arms take it in turns to pull through the water, balanced by the up and down leg kick.

Start learning back crawl by pushing off from the side into a back glide. Kick your legs up and down. Scull with your hands to keep your balance. Or, if you prefer, hold a float against your chest.

Kick your legs from the hips.

Back crawl arms

Look at the pictures of back crawl arm movements on the next page. The best way to learn them is to start off in a back glide kicking your legs. Try bringing each arm, in turn, up over your head and back through the water like a windmill. Keep practising and see how many arm pulls you can do.

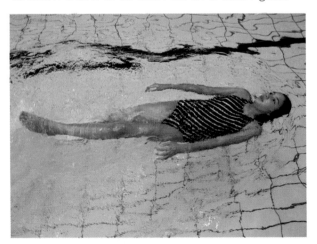 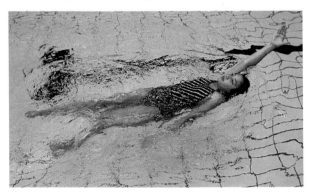

▲

Keep the continuous action going so that one arm is opposite the other all the time.

With back crawl, your face is out of the water all the time. The only problem is that you can't see where you are going – so always have a good look before you set off.

Leg movements

The leg kick used in back crawl is the same as for front crawl. The kick helps to keep your body flat and it balances the strong arm pull as well as pushing you along.

Arm Entry

Your hand and arm stretch behind your head and enter the water in line with your shoulder. Your hand enters little finger first, palm out.

Arm movements

There are two kinds of arm pull you can use in back crawl – STRAIGHT ARM and BENT ARM. Start by learning the straight arm one but the bent arm pull is faster, so you will need to learn this method if you wish to enter swimming races. Your arms enter the water the same way for both pulls.

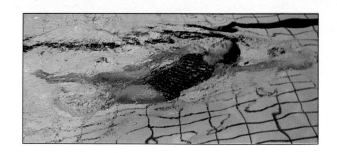

Bent arm pull

As you pull your arm through the water, your elbow bends. Then push your hand towards your feet stretching your arm straight. Lift your arm from the water, thumb first and return it to the entry position.

Straight arm pull

When your hand enters the water, little finger first, your arm is stretched behind your head. In the water your arm stays straight, pulling down and back. Push with your hand, towards your hip until the arm is straight down your side. Lift it, thumb first, out of the water and swing it up over your body ready to enter again.

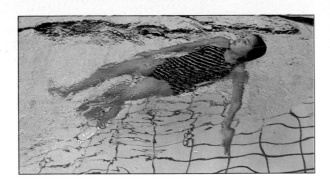

Keep your body as flat as possible.

LEARNING TO DIVE

Diving can be fun as a sport in its own right as well as a way of getting into the water. Once you can swim in deep water you are ready to learn how to dive.

Putting your head underwater

By now you should be used to putting your face in the water. Before you start diving, try these exercises to see what it's like having your whole head below the surface.

SAFETY

- Make sure you know which is the deep end and only dive at that end.
- Never dive into rivers or gravel pits as they might be shallow or full of dangerous objects.
- Protect your head by holding your hands as shown on the next page.

Hold on to the rail with one hand, take a deep breath and put your face right down into the water. Blow out lots of bubbles.

Push off from the side and glide to the bottom of the pool. Surface by raising your arms and pointing your hands upwards.

You can also try picking up objects from the bottom or swimming through someone's legs.

Sitting dive

Sit on the side of the pool with your feet together and resting on the rail at the edge. Bend forwards with your head down between outstretched arms. Lean forwards and you will topple over into a shallow dive.

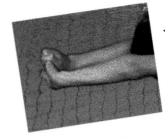

◄ When preparing to dive, link your hands together above your head, as shown in this picture.

Kneeling dive

Kneel down on one knee and curl the toes of your front foot round the edge of the pool. Stretch your arms up over your head and lean forward until you overbalance. Aim for the bottom of the pool and stretch your legs out behind as you go into the water. Glide back to the surface.

Crouch roll

Stand on the side of the pool with your feet together and your toes curling over the edge. Bend your knees and crouch down low.

Stretch your arms over your head, keeping your hands linked, and tuck your chin down on to your chest. Roll forwards and reach for the bottom of the pool.

►

Pike fall

Stand at the side of the pool with your feet together and toes gripping the edge. Keep your legs straight and bend at the waist. Press your arms close to your ears and hold your hands together.

Lean forward keeping your legs straight and eyes fixed on the water. Stretch your legs out behind you as you enter the water.

▲
Keep your head between your arms.

▲
Legs straight and toes pointed.

Springing dives

In springing dives, you push with your legs to dive into the water instead of toppling your body forwards as before. Try first doing a springing dive from a crouch position.

Crouch dive

Stand up straight with your toes curled over the edge of the pool. Stretch your arms up over your head and link your hands. Bend your knees, keeping your bottom tucked in.

Fix your eyes on the spot where you will enter the water. Spring up by straightening your legs and pushing off with your toes. As your hands touch the water, stretch your legs out and feel all the muscles in your body stretch as hard as they can.

Spring header

When you can do the crouch dive, try a "spring header". Begin with your legs straight and then bend, straighten and push off into the dive.

FUN AND GAMES

You can have a lot of fun trying out different ways of moving in the water, swimming to music and playing games such as ball. Try some of the ideas on these two pages in addition to practising your strokes. See also whether you can invent new strokes of your own.

Playing ball

You can play ball games in the pool as a complete beginner, keeping your feet on the bottom, or as a good swimmer in games such as water polo.

As a beginner, play catch with your teacher. If the ball lands out of your reach, try pushing off from the bottom of the pool and gliding on your front to get it. Kick your legs as they lift off the bottom. If you are swimming with friends, try "pig in the middle".

Once you can swim, play catch in the water where you

are just out of your depth. You will need to tread water (see page 9) when you are throwing or catching the ball. If you find this easy, see if you can throw and catch using one hand only. Can you swim keeping the ball out of the water?

If you enjoy playing ball games in the water, you could ask at your pool whether there is a water polo beginners team that you could join.

Water acrobatics

Try doing handstands on the bottom of the pool and somersaults under the water. The water will support your body, which makes these simple gymnastics much easier to do in water than on land.

Handstands

Do handstands in fairly shallow water. Take a deep breath, bend at your waist and reach for the bottom of the pool. Put your hands on the bottom, throw up your legs and stretch. See if you can walk on your hands along the bottom of the pool.

Somersaults

You can somersault forwards or backwards. To go forwards, float on your front, draw your knees up to your tummy and tuck your chin on to your chest. Pretend you are turning a skipping rope backwards and use your hands to paddle yourself round.

To somersault backwards, float on your back and get into the same tucked position as before, only this time turning backwards. Press down with outstretched hands and "skip" forwards.

GOING FURTHER

On pages 26 and 27 you can see how to play ball games and do simple acrobatics in the water, even before you can swim well. As your swimming gets better there are lots of other water sports you may want to try, (see opposite).

Below, you can find out a little about synchronized swimming and water polo. If you want to find out more, ask at your local pool for information on classes and training. Ask too if there is a swimming team or diving club you can join or other clubs where you can take part in such activities as canoeing, snorkelling or life-saving.

Synchronized swimming

Synchronized swimming is performing ballet-like movements and gymnastics in, on and under the water, in time to music. You can do it on your own, with a partner or with a team of people.

Each swimmer needs to control every stroke very carefully, sometimes swimming quickly, sometimes slowly, or treading water and making it all look graceful and easy. The music helps everybody to keep together and it is even played under the water so the swimmers can keep in time when they are below the surface.

Water polo

Water polo is a goal-scoring ball game played by two teams in a swimming pool. There are seven players in each team, including the goalkeeper. The object is to throw the ball into the other team's goal.

The ball can be pushed or thrown but you may only touch it with one hand and your feet must not touch the bottom. Only the goalkeeper can use both hands and stand to throw the ball.

World of Sports Photos

Thorpe Park

▲ **Water skiing**

Picturepoint – London

▲ **Surfing**

Ocean Optics Ltd

▲ **Scuba diving**

Picturepoint – London

▲ **Snorkelling**

Picturepoint – London

Picturepoint – London

◀ **Windsurfing**   **Canoeing** ▲

29

WATER SAFETY

Accidents can happen, even to very good swimmers, but if you follow a few simple rules when you are at the pool, at the seaside or near rivers, canals and lakes you can help stop accidents happening and enjoy the water in safety.

At the pool

Don't run by the pool.
You might slip and hurt yourself or knock a non-swimmer into the water.

Don't push people in.
They may not be able to swim, or they might bang their head on the side or hurt someone by landing on them.

Don't push people or hold them under water.
You might scare them, or choke them.

Don't eat sweets or chew gum when swimming.
If they stick in your throat you might choke and get into difficulties.

Do make sure there is no one in the way before you jump or dive in.

Outside

Don't ever swim alone.
If you have problems, strangers might not notice.

Don't fool around near rivers, lakes, canals or quaysides.
If you fall in, it may be very difficult to get out again.

Don't play with rescue and safety equipment.
Someone may drown if it is missing or damaged.

Do wear a life jacket if you go out in a small boat.

Do take care when using air beds and inflatable boats.
Strong winds and tides can sweep you out to sea very fast.

SWIMMING AWARDS

There are lots of different swimming awards you can work towards in your lessons. The Amateur Swimming Association (ASA), The Swimming Teachers' Association (STA), and the Royal Life Saving Society (RLSS) are three of the organizations who run award schemes and below you can see just some of the badges you can earn.

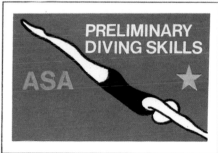

If you have started diving, playing water polo or doing synchronized swimming you will find that there are badges for all of these skills and as your swimming gets stronger you can learn how to rescue people from the water and get your life-saving badges too.

The awards are for every level of swimmer. Some test how far you can swim, some test your speed or style or water safety and some test all your skills in the water.

Your swimming teacher or the swimming coach at your local pool will be able to tell you about the awards you can take and will suggest which one you are ready to work for.

INDEX

This edition published 1994 by Diamond Books
77–85 Fulham Palace Road
Hammersmith, London W6 8JB

First published 1990
© text HarperCollinsPublishers 1990

ISBN 0 261 66 466-2

Set in 12/14 Helvetica
Printed and bound in Italy

Mr. Yowder and the Giant Bull Snake

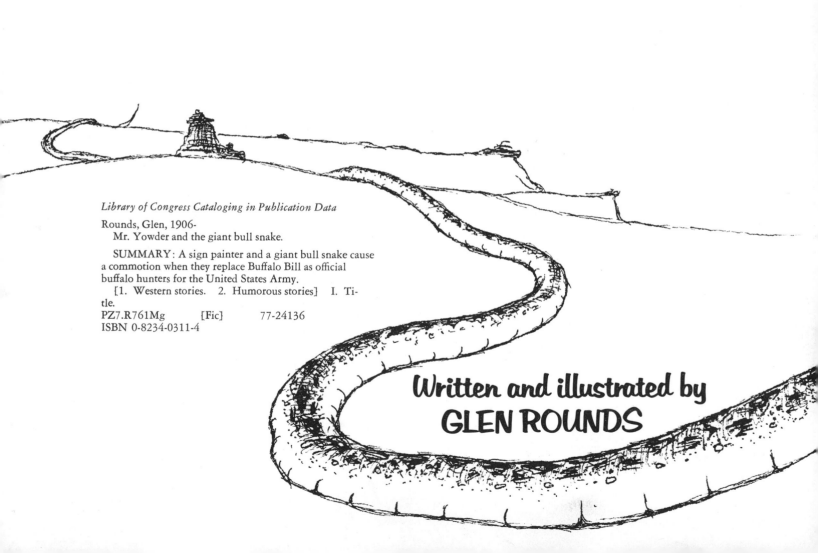

Library of Congress Cataloging in Publication Data

Rounds, Glen, 1906-
   Mr. Yowder and the giant bull snake.

   SUMMARY: A sign painter and a giant bull snake cause
a commotion when they replace Buffalo Bill as official
buffalo hunters for the United States Army.
   [1. Western stories. 2. Humorous stories] I. Ti-
tle.
PZ7.R761Mg   [Fic]   77-24136
ISBN 0-8234-0311-4

Written and illustrated by
GLEN ROUNDS

Mr. Yowder and the Giant Bull Snake

Holiday House, New York

At the time I speak of (which was a long time ago), that part of the country known as THE GREAT PLAINS was still mostly uninhabited.

An occasional adventurous settler plowed up small patches of sod fenced in with barbed wire, Indians chased buffalo—or the settlers' livestock—and were themselves chased by soldiers.

But in that vast treeless land such scattered activities went almost unnoticed, and the general impression was of a place where nobody lived and where nothing ever happened.

It seemed an unlikely place to find a sign painter, but nonetheless Mr. Xenon Zebulon Yowder, who even then spoke of himself as "The World's Bestest and Fastest Sign Painter," was there. He wasn't going anywhere in particular, just taking himself a trip to see the country.

When he ran short of flour, coffee, or other supplies, he'd join one of the wagon trains crossing the plains on the way to Oregon or California and paint PIKES PEAK OR BUST, WE ARE FROM OHIO, and other such sayings in fancy letters on the wagons in return for what he needed.

Other times he made a little money painting road signs pointing to water holes, short cuts, or good camping places.

But mostly he rode alone, just exploring the country and thinking of the stories he'd have to tell later.

One afternoon, near the headwaters of The Powder River—or maybe it was Pumpkin Creek (he had no map and couldn't be right sure)—Mr. Yowder shot two fat prairie hens and made camp by a small clear spring. After picketing his horse on good grass, he'd built a fire, put the birds on to cook and was leaning back against his saddle, taking a rest, when he first noticed the little snake.

As was usual for that time of year—it was late spring by the way—hundreds of newly hatched bull snakes were going about their business in the tall grass, learning the bull snake trade. And now one of these had come up to the other side of the fire and was investigating Mr. Yowder's bedding roll.

Mr. Yowder liked all sorts of animals, even snakes, so he watched as this one tested and tasted each string and strap with his flickering forked tongue.

But when the snake started to crawl inside the blanket roll, he spoke up. "You'd better stay out of that, Snake," he said in snake. "That there's my bed."

The little snake was somewhat startled by hearing a man speaking his language, and scuttled into the grass. But he quickly returned, stuck his head up and asked, "Where did you learn to talk snake?"

"I worked one time down in Oklahoma territory, painting signs along the 'Strip,'" Mr. Yowder told him. "Were a sight of snakes there, and almost no people, so if I wanted anybody to talk to, I had to learn snake."

That seemed reasonable to the little bull snake, and he curled up by the fire to listen to Mr. Yowder's tales of the places he'd been and the strange things he'd seen.

When the birds were cooked Mr. Yowder ate his supper, now and then cutting off small slivers of meat for the snake, who now was busily telling how dull bull snake life was thereabouts. He explained that he was ambitious—which was unusual for a snake—and he hoped to see the world and maybe become famous when he was bigger.

Mr. Yowder was impressed, but he couldn't see much chance for a snake to become famous out in that county.

All in all, however, they both enjoyed the talk, and just before dark the little bull snake went off home to bed, his head full of the stories Mr. Yowder had told him.

Out on the plain nearby was a high rock—a landmark that could be seen for miles—and Mr. Yowder spent nearly a week painting YOWDER THE SIGN PAINTER WAS HERE in large fancy letters up near the top of it. That sign, though faded by wind and rain, could still be read by passersby until about eight years ago.

And every afternoon when Mr. Yowder came back to camp, the little snake was there to meet him. One day Mr. Yowder said to him, "It don't seem right to just keep calling you 'Snake.' You need a name. So if you don't mind, I'm going to call you Knute, after my old uncle back in Missouri."

Of course the snake was right pleased, for none of his friends or relations had names, or even nicknames.

Sitting by the small fire, the man and the snake would talk for hours, or Mr. Yowder would read aloud from some tattered magazines he had in his pack. The snake liked Western stories, but best of all he liked the magazine that told of people who started out puny but later took body-building courses and became so strong no bully ever again dared kick sand in their faces. Over and over, he had Mr. Yowder read him the story of how Mr. Teddy Roosevelt took exercises and became President of the United States.

When Knute suggested that maybe Mr. Yowder could send off and get him one of those body-building courses, Mr. Yowder explained to him that, there being no post offices on the Great Plains as yet, it would be difficult to either send or receive mail. Besides, those courses were probably pretty expensive.

But when he saw how disappointed Knute was, he suggested that, exercise being the main part of body-building, maybe between them they could invent some of their own.

For a start he pointed to two tall weeds standing about the snake's length apart, and showed Knute how to hook his neck around one, and take a hitch with his tail around the other. Then he told him to flex all his muscles and try to pull the tops together, relax, then pull again.

In a few minutes the snake was out of breath, not being used to any exercise more violent than wriggling through the grass, hunting for birds' eggs, grasshoppers, and other small game. He dropped to the ground, and for a while lay panting.

The next day the little snake's muscles were stiff and sore, and Mr. Yowder expected him to give up the body-building idea then and there. But Knute was indeed an unusual snake, and hour after hour—while his friends and relatives took naps, or lay about in the sun—he did his exercises.

All that exercise, however, gave him a tremendous appetite. So when he wasn't exercising he was hunting for something to eat, and he began to grow faster than any snake on the Great Plains. Every afternoon, near sundown, he would make a full-length impression of his body on a patch of white sand near his den to mark the progress of his body-building.

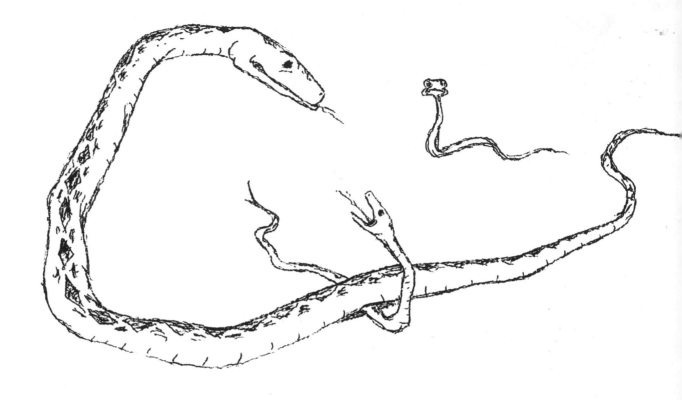

By the time Mr. Yowder began to think of drifting south to find work for the winter, Knute was already many times larger than any snake in the neighborhood. And he told Mr. Yowder that the others had begun to complain that he was all the time running over them, knocking them down, spraining their backs, or kicking dust in their eyes.

So, much as he disliked the idea of leaving home, it looked as if he'd have to find a place where there was more room for a snake his size.

Knute was very good company, and Mr. Yowder enjoyed having someone to talk to. Besides that, he caught his own food. So Mr. Yowder suggested that they travel south together. The snake was pleased by the chance to see the world. While Mr. Yowder saddled his horse and rolled up his camp outfit, Knute went to tell his friends and relations good-bye. He said he'd try to let them know if he found work, and the last they ever saw of him he was racing along beside Mr. Yowder's horse.

Mr. Yowder was in no hurry, so Knute had plenty of time to hunt for food and to keep up his body-building exercises as well. Before they rode into any of the small towns along the way, Mr. Yowder would take the snake up and hang him from the saddle horn like a coil of old rope. That saved them much trouble from dogs, constables, and people who simply disliked snakes.

At Abilene, Kansas—or maybe it was Dodge City—Mr. Yowder decided they were far enough south. He and the snake moved into an abandoned shack a mile or so out of town and settled down for the winter.

Every morning after breakfast Mr. Yowder let Knute out to hunt in the open country to the west, while he himself spent the day in town, painting signs or playing cards.

By Christmas, however, Mr. Yowder began to wonder if maybe he hadn't made a mistake starting Knute on the body-building idea. For the snake continued to grow, and by Groundhog Day was so long that, by the time he had looped and coiled himself around inside the shack, getting himself comfortable for the night, there was very little room left for Mr. Yowder. And there was also the danger that he might accidentally knock over the stove or upset the lantern and set the place afire.

But luckily spring came early, and Mr. Yowder and the snake went back to camping on the prairie as they'd done before. Mr. Yowder got a job with the railroad, painting numbers on mileposts and names on the little stations along the tracks.

While Mr. Yowder worked, Knute hunted and exercised as usual. But in the afternoons he liked to lie with his body out of sight behind a low hill, his chin resting flat on the crest, and watch the long trains go puffing by.

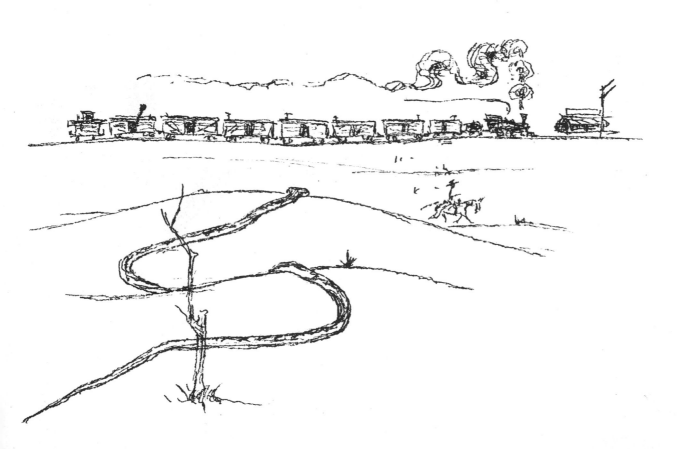

Things went well enough with Mr. Yowder and the snake during the early spring, until the night a violent thunder and lightning storm stampeded a trail herd of Texas longhorns being held nearby. The cattle missed Mr. Yowder's camp, but in the excitement his horse got loose and was never seen again.

Mr. Yowder disliked the idea of walking to his work, so one day he asked Knute if he'd mind trying the saddle on for size. The snake didn't mind, and Mr. Yowder strapped it on the snake's neck, just behind his head. When the man had his feet in the stirrups, the snake raised his head and they went for a short ride. The saddle fit just fine.

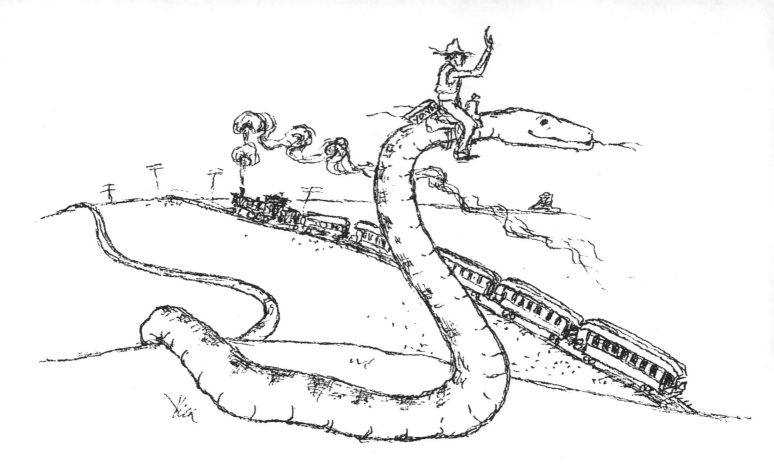

Every morning after that, Mr. Yowder rode to wherever he was working, then turned Knute loose to hunt, after telling him where to meet him at quitting time.

At first the train crews were a little startled by the sight of Mr. Yowder riding along beside the tracks on the giant snake, but they soon got used to the idea and always waved when they went by.

However, Easterners, politicians, and other such folk never did quite believe their eyes.

Knute was living almost entirely on buffalo by then, and when he had time Mr. Yowder often rode along while the snake did his day's hunting. After Knute had fed, if Mr. Yowder needed meat for himself or to give to his friends among the train crews, he would shoot a fat buffalo and carry the meat home strapped behind his saddle.

The snake had a smooth gait and, shooting from his high perch, Mr. Yowder seldom missed.

One day, on the way back from one of their hunts, Mr. Yowder and Knute came over a low hill and met a patrol of the soldiers who usually spent all of their time chasing Indians around the country. The soldiers had never seen so large a snake, nor even heard tell of one, so they and their horses were considerably upset.

But after Mr. Yowder dismounted and had Knute back down the slope out of sight, both men and horses quieted down. The General in command had heard stories about the man and the snake who hunted buffalo, and now he walked up to shake hands with Mr. Yowder and get a closer look at Knute.

The General was a man who was seldom surprised by anything, but even so he could hardly believe his ears when he heard Mr. Yowder and Knute talking snake.

After his first surprise, the General got right down to business, as is the way with generals. It seemed that Mr. Buffalo Bill, who was the Army's official buffalo hunter, had joined a wild West show and gone back East and other places. So the fort was running out of meat, and the General had had to put most of his soldiers to work hunting buffalo.

But it turned out the soldiers were not very good buffalo hunters. They talked loud, and the rattling of their spurs, sabers, and other gear often frightened herds a half a mile away. And when they did get close, they found that their cavalry horses panicked at the sight and smell of buffalo. So, what with one thing and another, the cooks at the fort still had almost nothing to cook, and the soldiers were beginning to complain.

Besides that, with the soldiers spending all of their time trying to shoot buffalo, there was nobody left to chase the Indians. So they were getting fat and lazy, spending their time in their tepees taking naps, telling stories, or gambling. And of course the Government didn't like that. So what the General wanted was to hire Mr. Yowder and the snake to take Mr. Buffalo Bill's place hunting buffalo for the Army so the soldiers could get back to chasing Indians, which was what they were being paid for.

Mr. Yowder told the General things were a little slow in the sign painting business right then and, as far as he was concerned, he'd be pleased to help the Army out. But naturally he'd have to talk it over with the snake first.

After Mr. Yowder had explained to him what the General had in mind, Knute thought for a while and decided he sort of liked the idea of being the only snake in the world working for the Government. So he and Mr. Yowder took Mr. Buffalo Bill's place as official buffalo hunters for the United States Army.

It was a grand sight to see them leave for work of a morning. No matter how early the hour or bad the weather the General, in his nightshirt, stood by the fort gates to wave good-bye. Behind the General the band would be playing "Garry Owen," "The Yellow Rose of Texas," and other loud tunes that soldiers like.

The mule teams pulling the line of wagons that would haul the meat back, and the horses of the butchers and buffalo skinners who rode alongside, stirred up a cloud of dust that almost hid Knute as he moved along the column. The great snake arched his neck like a proud horse, while Mr. Yowder sat straight in his saddle, holding his favorite buffalo gun in one hand and the staff of the flag the General had given them in the other.

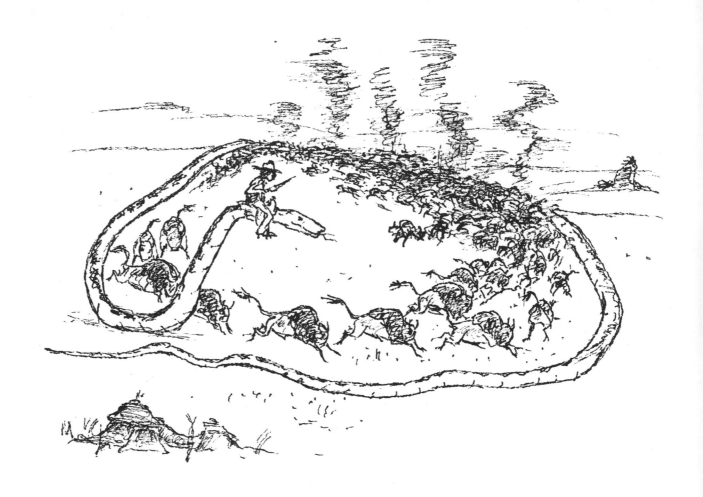

As soon as they were out of sight of the fort, Knute and Mr. Yowder would go on ahead while the wagons followed, for the snake traveled much faster than the horses and mules. When they found buffalo, Knute would circle the herd, completely hemming it in, while Mr. Yowder sat in the saddle and shot as many as the Army wagons could haul away.

When that was done, Mr. Yowder would build a little fire and pile a bunch of green sage on it to make a smoke signal to guide the wagons following them. Then he and Knute would stretch out on the grass and rest until the butchers and skinners had finished their work. Later, when the wagons were loaded down with meat and hides, the man and snake would lead the way back to the fort.

It was a good job, and Knute and Mr. Yowder might have been working for the Army yet, but Mr. Buffalo Bill got tired of the wild West show (the long hours and all) and asked for his job back, hunting buffalo for the Army.

The General knew that Knute and Mr. Yowder were really bringing in more meat than Mr. Buffalo Bill had done. But on the other hand, Mr. Buffalo Bill was now a very famous person, and he had just explained to the General that the President of the United States—who was a personal friend of Mr. Buffalo Bill's—along with a trainload of senators, governors, and newspaper writers, was coming out to the fort the very next day to watch Mr. Buffalo Bill shoot buffalo. A general, if he wants to keep on being a general, needs to be friendly to such people, so he told Mr. Yowder and Knute he was sorry but he'd have to pay them off.

Mr. Yowder and the snake went back to their camp behind the fort to talk things over. Nobody had told them that the President of the United States was coming to the fort to watch Mr. Buffalo Bill shoot buffalo the next day. But the General had paid them for the full week, even though it was only Friday—and they felt they owed the Government the extra day's work they had already been paid for.

So early the next morning, without saying anything to anybody, they set off by themselves on their last day's work for the Government.

About midmorning, Mr. Yowder and Knute found the biggest buffalo herd they'd ever seen—they couldn't guess how many, but there must have been thousands, or maybe a million—on the head of Sand Creek, some miles beyond the Box Elder. This time they had no wagons along, or men to skin the buffalo and load the meat, so they decided to slowly drive the whole herd right up to the gate of the fort before Mr. Yowder started shooting.

It was a little before noon when the President of the United States and his party drove out from town. They shook hands with Mr. Buffalo Bill, were introduced to the General, and listened to a short band concert. Then one of Mr. Buffalo Bill's Indian scouts rode up on a sweaty horse, saying a herd of buffalo was just coming into the wide valley of Box Elder Creek only a couple of miles away.

Mr. Buffalo Bill mounted his white horse, waved his favorite buffalo gun over his head, and told the President of the United States and the other important people to get into the wagons and follow him to the top of the nearby ridge, where there would be a good view of the herd. As soon as they were in place, he'd show them how he, The Greatest Buffalo Hunter in the United States of America, and perhaps the greatest in the world, went about his work.

Little did Mr. Buffalo Bill know that the buffalo herd was being driven by Knute and Mr. Yowder. Nor did he know that a piece of paper blowing in the grass had just stampeded the herd.

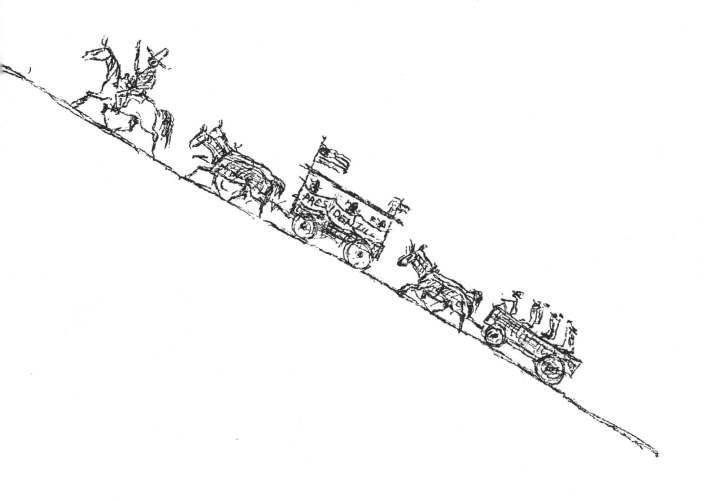

And directly in the path of those thousands of maddened beasts were Mr. Buffalo Bill, himself, and the President of the United States, as well as all the other important people!

When the leaders of the stampeding herd roared over the ridge ahead of him, Mr. Buffalo Bill did his best, but as soon as he shot one a hundred more took its place. The huge dust cloud hid what was happening, and all one could hear was the bellowing of buffalo, the shouting of men (the President's voice loudest of all), the thunder of buffalo hooves, and the breaking of wood as the wagons were overturned and trampled into kindling.

How long the stampede lasted nobody remembers, but when Knute and Mr. Yowder looked over the ridge into the slowly settling cloud of dust, they

saw broken, overturned wagons, runaway horses, and torn flags and strips of
bunting scattered over the slopes below. Mr. Buffalo Bill, his white hat black
with dust, was stamping about, waving his hands and kicking at the dead buffalo
lying about.

The General and a couple of governors were dusting the President of the
United States off, pinning up the rips in his coat, and trying to find his hat. But
nobody was badly hurt, and Mr. Yowder saw there was really nothing he could
do to help, so he and Knute quietly turned around and went back the way
they'd come.

Neither Mr. Yowder nor the giant bull snake were ever seen in those parts again. Some say that Knute finally settled in South America, where large snakes are not uncommon. Others have it that he went East and got into the sea serpent business—but nobody knows for sure.

Mr. Yowder later became famous as The World's Fastest and Bestest Sign Painter, but it is a well known fact that he never after that talked snake. Nor did he ever again have dealings with the United States Army.